Community Helpers

Counselors

by Erika S. Manley

Bullfrog
Books

Ideas for Parents and Teachers

Bullfrog Books let children practice reading informational text at the earliest reading levels. Repetition, familiar words, and photo labels support early readers.

Before Reading

- Discuss the cover photo. What does it tell them?

- Look at the picture glossary together. Read and discuss the words.

Read the Book

- "Walk" through the book and look at the photos. Let the child ask questions. Point out the photo labels.

- Read the book to the child, or have him or her read independently.

After Reading

- Prompt the child to think more. Ask: Have you heard about counselors before reading this book? What more would you like to learn about them after reading it?

Bullfrog Books are published by Jump!
5357 Penn Avenue South
Minneapolis, MN 55419
www.jumplibrary.com

Library of Congress Cataloging-in-Publication Data

Names: Manley, Erika S., author.
Title: Counselors / by Erika S. Manley.
Description: Minneapolis, MN: Jump!, Inc., 2020.
Series: Community helpers | Includes index.
Audience: Age 5–8. | Audience: K to Grade 3.
Identifiers: LCCN 2018055996 (print)
LCCN 2019002845 (ebook)
ISBN 9781641288309 (ebook)
ISBN 9781641288286 (hardcover : alk. paper)
ISBN 9781641288293 (pbk.)
Subjects: LCSH: Counselors—Juvenile literature.
Listening—Juvenile literature.
Classification: LCC BF636.6 (ebook)
LCC BF636.6 .M365 2020 (print) | DDC 158.1—dc23
LC record available at https://lccn.loc.gov/2018055996

Editor: Jenna Trnka
Design: Shoreline Publishing Group

Photo Credits: Katarzyna Bialasiewicz/iStock, cover; Robert Kneschke/Dreamstime, 1; Racobovt/Shutterstock, 3; Rido/Shutterstock, 4; Andrey Popov/Dreamstime, 5; Monkey Business Images/Dreamstime, 6–7, 23br; Pressmaster/Dreamstime, 8; Pressmaster/Shutterstock, 9, 10–11; Fizkes/Shutterstock, 12–13; Evgeny Atamanenko/Dreamstime, 14–15; Iam Anupong/Shutterstock, 16, 17, 23tr; Valerii Honcharuk/Alamy, 18–19, 23bl; Steve Debenport/iStock, 20 21; New Africa/Shutterstock, 22; Wavebreakmedia/Shutterstock, 23tl; Billion Photos/Shutterstock, 24.

Printed in the United States of America at Corporate Graphics in North Mankato, Minnesota.

Table of Contents

Good Listeners

Kyle wants to be a counselor.

What do they do?

They listen.

They are trained.
They ask good
questions.
They offer
solutions, too.

6

Eva is bullied.

Not nice!

Eva talks to Ted.

Ted works at school.
He helps. How?
He talks to the bullies.

9

The bullies
say sorry.

Eva feels better.

Emma is mad.

Why?

Troy asks her.

He helps her calm down.

Kate is new at school.

She is scared.

Eli answers her questions.

He takes her to class.

Nice!

Ben finds it hard to focus.

Jean helps.

He finishes his homework!

homework

17

Elle is nervous around new people.

AJ helps.

How?

She says it is OK to ask for space.

Elle feels better!

Counselors do good work!

At the Counselor's Office

office
A counselor's office is private.
This helps the counselor listen.

books
Counselors have
books we can
read together or
alone to help us.

couch
Comfortable chairs and furniture
help people feel comfortable
when talking to the counselor.

games and toys
Games and toys
help us relax in the
counselor's office.
They help us learn,
interact, and
communicate, too.

Picture Glossary

bullied
Treated in a cruel, insulting, or threatening way.

focus
To concentrate.

nervous
Anxious or worried.

solutions
Answers to or ways to solve problems.

23

Index

To Learn More

Finding more information is as easy as 1, 2, 3.

❶ Go to www.factsurfer.com

❷ Enter "counselors" into the search box.

❸ Choose your book to see a list of websites.